TH
BRENDAN
BEHAN
QUOTATION BOOK

THE
BRENDAN
BEHAN
QUOTATION BOOK

Compiled by Andrew Russell

SOMERVILLE PRESS

Somerville Press Ltd,
Dromore, Bantry,
Co. Cork, Ireland

First published 2015

Front cover photo: © Getty Images.

Designed by Jane Stark
Typeset in Minion Pro
seamistgraphics@gmail.com

ISBN: 978 0 9927364 4 6

Printed in the EU

INTRODUCTION

BRENDAN BEHAN was born in Dublin in 1923 into a working-class, Republican but artistic family. When he was eight years old he joined Fianna Éireann, the junior branch of the IRA, and it was while was in borstal in England for taking part in an IRA bombing campaign, that he started writing.

His autobiographical novel *Borstal Boy,* which he commenced in 1941, was highly regarded by Sean O'Faolain, editor of *The Bell*, but was not published until 1958.

His play, *The Quare Fellow* (1954), which highlights the barbarity of capital punishment, was originally produced in the experimental Pike Theatre in Dublin, having been turned down by both the Abbey Theatre and the Gate Theatre. It was its successful production by Joan Litttlewood in London that made Behan famous.

The Hostage (1958), generally considered to be his finest play, was first produced in Irish as *An Giall* in Dublin.

Largely due to his lifestyle, he produced little written work after that, although his two taped reminiscences *Brendan Behan's Island* (1962) and *Brendan Behan's New York* (1964) were both successful.

Richard's Cork Leg, was unfinished at the time of his death, but was later staged in the Peacock Theatre in Dublin (1972).

Brendan Behan was married to Beatrice ffrench-Salkeld and died in Dublin in 1964.

IF IT'S A THING
I GO FOR
IN A HUMAN BEING,
IT'S WEAKNESS.

I'M A DEVIL FOR IT.

IN MY WORK,

I TRY TO MIRROR

WHAT HAPPENS

TO THE PEOPLE INVOLVED

AND LEAVE IT TO THE

LITERARY INTELLIGENTSIA

TO EXPOUND THEIR OWN

THEORIES AFTERWARDS.

I MUST ADMIT,
I STILL PREFER TO LIVE IN IRELAND,
ALTHOUGH I HAVE GREAT ADMIRATION
FOR THE BRITISH PEOPLE.

NO ONE BUT THEY WOULD HAVE USED
CHURCHILL DURING THE WAR
AND THEN
THROWN HIM OUT
AT THE RIGHT TIME
AFTERWARDS.

I SPEND MOST OF MY TIME
WITH NON-LITERARY FELLOWS
THAT I HAVE KNOWN
FROM MY YOUTH.
I LIKE CITY PEOPLE
FROM DUBLIN OR
FROM THE EAST END.

HUNGER
MAKES
PORNOGRAPHERS
OF US
ALL.

THE POLITICIAN
WHO INTRODUCED
THE HOLY HOUR
TO THE DÁIL
WAS SHOT DEAD
AN HOUR
AFTERWARDS.

I HAVE A MIND
THAT WOULD BURST
RATHER THAN SUSTAIN
A MOOD OR SUBJECT
FOR LONG.

ANYONE WHO
MAKES CAPITAL
OUT OF
ACTS OF VIOLENCE
AND HATRED
IS A FOOL.

SUCCESS IS DAMN NEAR
KILLING ME.

IF I HAD MY WAY,
I WOULD PRESCRIBE THAT
SUCCESS SHOULD
GO TO EVERY MAN
FOR A MONTH:

THEN HE WOULD BE GIVEN A
PENSION AND FORGOTTEN.

I RESPECT KINDNESS TO
HUMAN BEINGS FIRST OF ALL,
AND KINDNESS TO ANIMALS.
I DON'T RESPECT THE LAW:
I HAVE A TOTAL IRREVERENCE
FOR ANYTHING CONNECTED WITH
SOCIETY EXCEPT THAT WHICH MAKES
THE ROADS SAFER,
THE BEER STRONGER,
THE FOOD CHEAPER,
AND OLD MEN AND OLD WOMEN
WARMER IN THE WINTER
AND HAPPIER IN THE SUMMER.

I HAVE BEEN
VERY PATRIOTIC
DURING MY STAY IN
HER MAJESTY'S PRISON.
I WILL ONLY SPEAK
IRISH.

ONLY A LUNATIC
BOASTS OF TAKING
A HUMAN LIFE.
ESSENTIALLY
I'M A GENTLE
AND AMIABLE
PERSON.

THE ART OF CONVERSATION

IS GONE,

MURDERED BY LUNATICS,

MOST OF THEM

IN THE UNITED STATES.

WHENEVER I TRAVEL
ANYWHERE
IN A PLANE,
IT SEEMS TO BE
FULL OF NUNS.
AND THEY TAKE THE
VOW OF POVERTY.

I'M NOT A POLITICIAN
BECAUSE I HAVE
ONLY ONE FACE.

•

WHEN I'M SICK
I'M VERY RELIGIOUS.

BEATNIKS –
THE THING I HAVE
AGAINST THEM IS
THAT THEY ARE
ALWAYS LOOKING
FOR A JOB – MY JOB.

I'VE NEVER FELT SO MUCH
AT HOME ANYWHERE
THAN I DO IN
NEW YORK.

•

THE FIRST DUTY
OF A WRITER IS TO
LET HIS COUNTRY DOWN.

PEOPLE WHO SAY
MANUAL LABOUR
IS A GOOD THING
HAVE NEVER DONE ANY.

THE HEBREWS
AND THE GAELS
HAVE MUCH IN COMMON.
BOTH ARE EXOTIC ENOUGH
TO BE INTERESTING
AND FOREIGN ENOUGH
TO BE ALARMING.

A TYPICAL BEHAN COSTUME

IS A

BROOKS BROTHERS SUIT

WITH TWO BUTTONS OFF

AND

A BIG BOOZE STAIN

ON THE FRONT.

WHO NEEDS
FOCKIN' TEETH?

I TOOK MINE OUT
AND THREW THEM
IN THE LIFFEY.

WHEN DEAN SWIFT SPOKE IN
ST PATRICK'S CATHEDRAL
IN DUBLIN,
THE ONLY ONE THERE
WAS HIS BUTLER.

SO SWIFT BEGAN
'DEARLY BELOVED PATRICK'.

I KNOW I'M HAPPIEST
WHEN I'M WRITING.

•

I NEVER WROTE WHILE DRINKING.

•

ALCOHOL
IS THE
ENEMY OF THE WRITER.

THE MORE FAMOUS I HAVE BECOME THE MORE ENEMIES I SEEM TO HAVE.

I HAVE A NEW THEORY
ABOUT WHAT HAPPENED
TO THE SNAKES WHEN
ST PATRICK DROVE THEM
OUT OF IRELAND.

THEY CAME TO
NEW YORK
AND BECAME JUDGES.

I CAN'T READ A NOTE OF MUSIC
BUT I CAN CERTAINLY READ
A CHEQUE.

•

CANADA IS BARBARIC
WITHOUT BEING PICTURESQUE.

•

IN MY PRIVATE LIFE
I'M A RATHER GLOOMY PERSON.

THERE IS NOTHING
I WOULD RATHER DO
THAN WRITE—
EXCEPT TALK IN
PUBS, RESTAURANTS,
BISTROS, SALOONS.

HOWEVER YOU GET
NO $ OR £ FOR THAT.

FOLK-SINGERS
I PERSONALLY DETEST.

I WOULD SHOOT
EVERY ONE OF THEM.

•

I'M A DRINKER
WITH WRITING PROBLEMS.

CRITICS ARE LIKE

EUNUCHS IN A HAREM:

THEY KNOW HOW IT'S DONE,

THEY'VE SEEN IT DONE EVERY DAY,

BUT

THEY'RE UNABLE

TO DO IT THEMSELVES.

SINCE I WAS A CHILD
I'VE HAD A
PATHOLOGICAL HORROR
OF COUNTRY PEOPLE.

•

THE FREEDOM OF IRELAND
IS TO ME
A SECOND RELIGION.

LIMERICK GIRLS
ARE VERY CAREFUL ABOUT
KEEPING THEIR LEGS SHUT,
IF NOT THEIR MOUTHS.

THE ENGLISH ARE
EVEN MORE
SUBTLE LIARS
THAN WE ARE.

•

THE IRISH ARE
A VERY POPULAR RACE
—WITH THEMSELVES.

I TOOK UP WRITING
BECAUSE IT'S EASIER THAN
HOUSE PAINTING.

•

THE KEY TO READING *ULYSSES*
IS TO TREAT IT LIKE A COMEDIAN
—AS A SORT OF GAG BOOK.

THE NUMBER OF PEOPLE
WHO BUY BOOKS IN IRELAND
WOULD NOT KEEP ME IN DRINK
FOR THE DURATION OF
THE SUNDAY OPENING TIME.

YOU WOULDN'T BE MINDING
THEM POET FELLOWS,
THEY'RE A
DANGEROUS CLIQUE
AT THE BEST OF TIMES.

•

THERE'S NO BAD PUBLICITY
EXCEPT AN OBITUARY.

IT'S NOT THAT
THE IRISH ARE CYNICAL.

IT'S RATHER THEY HAVE A
WONDERFUL
LACK OF RESPECT
FOR EVERYTHING
AND EVERYBODY.

THEY TOOK AWAY
OUR LAND,
OUR LANGUAGE,
AND OUR RELIGION:

BUT THEY COULD
NEVER HARNESS
OUR TONGUES.

I HAVE NEVER SEEN
A SITUATION
SO DISMAL THAT
A POLICEMAN
COULD NOT
MAKE IT WORSE.

I SAW A SIGN
WHICH SAID
'DRINK CANADA DRY'.

SO I DID.

IT'S A QUEER WORLD,
GOD KNOWS,
BUT THE BEST WE HAVE
TO BE GOING ON WITH.

THE BIG DIFFERENCE

BETWEEN

SEX FOR MONEY

AND

SEX FOR FREE

IS THAT

SEX FOR MONEY

USUALLY COSTS A LOT LESS.

OTHER PEOPLE HAVE
A NATIONALITY.

THE IRISH AND THE JEWS HAVE
A PSYCHOSIS.

I ONLY TAKE DRINK
ON TWO OCCASIONS—
WHEN I'M THIRSTY
AND
WHEN I'M NOT.

IF IT WAS
RAINING SOUP,
THE IRISH
WOULD GO OUT
WITH FORKS.

It is a good deed
to forget a poor joke.

•

Ah, bless you Sister,
may all your sons
be bishops.

THE MOST IMPORTANT
THINGS IN THE WORLD ARE
TO GET SOMETHING TO EAT,
SOMETHING TO DRINK
AND
SOMEBODY TO LOVE YOU.

•

I AM DAYLIGHT ATHEIST.

New York is my Lourdes,
where I go for
my spiritual refreshment
...a place where
you're least likely
to be bitten by a wild goat.

I SUPPOSE I AM INCLINED
TO BELIEVE IN ALL THAT THE
CATHOLIC CHURCH TEACHES.

●

I HAVE NOTHING AGAINST
THE CHURCH AS LONG AS
THEY LEAVE THE DRINK ALONE.

I AM ACCUSED
OF BEING
BLASPHEMOUS.

BUT BLASPHEMY IS
THE COMIC VERSE
OF BELIEF.

ANYTHING
WRITTEN IN JAIL
IS RUBBISH.

AND THAT INCLUDES
PILGRIM'S PROGRESS.

I ENJOY SMOKING
EXPENSIVE CIGARS
MADE IN CUBA
BY CASTRO.

YOU CAN FEEL
RADICAL AND BOURGEOIS
AT THE SAME TIME.

I LIKE NUNS
BETTER THAN
PRIESTS.

•

I'VE ALWAYS BEEN
INTERESTED IN
LOSERS.

THE CONVERSATION
OF THE
BRITISH UPPER CLASSES
IS RATHER SHOCKING
TO ANYONE
WHO'S NOT USED TO IT.

I LIKE IT.

DUBLIN
IS A CITY WHERE THERE'S
FAMILIARITY WITHOUT FRIENDSHIP,
LONELINESS WITHOUT SOLITUDE.

O'CASEY TOLD ME
TO STOP DRINKING.
'WHY?' I ASKED.
'BECAUSE YOU HAVE
WORK TO DO,'
HE REPLIED.

I THINK HE'S RIGHT.

THE MOST
IMPORTANT THING
IN LIFE,
AS I SEE IT,
IS TO REMAIN IN
A STATE OF
GOOD HUMOUR.

JOYCE AND O'CASEY
WERE THE WRITERS THAT
INFLUENCED ME MOST.

•

MY ONE AMBITION
IS TO LIVE
AS LONG AS I CAN.

TO PRAISE
O'CASEY
IS LIKE PRAISING THE
NIAGARA FALLS.
THERE ARE NO WORDS
TO DESCRIBE IT.

THE
SOLITARY
CONFINEMENT
NEAR DROVE ME CRAZY.

I WAS NEVER
MADE TO BE ALONE.

IF YOU FIGHT FOR THE
LIBERTY AND UNITY
OF A SMALL COUNTRY
—YOU'RE AN ANARCHIST:
BUT IF YOU GO BOMBING
FOR A GREAT POWER,
YOU'RE A PATRIOT.

IT ALL DEPENDS ON THE SIZE
OF THE COUNTRY IN QUESTION.

BIGOD,
I'D RATHER BE DEAD
THAN THINK ABOUT DEATH.

SURE IF I
TOOK NOTICE
OF MY CRITICS,
I'D BE IN A
MENTAL HOME
LONG AGO.

I'M PREPARED TO DIE,
IF NECESSARY,
FOR FRANCE
BUT NOT FOR
AIR FRANCE.

THE ONLY PEOPLE
I EVER MET
WHO BELIEVED IN
CAPITAL PUNISHMENT
WERE
MURDERERS.

KILLING YOUR WIFE
IS A NATURAL CLASS
OF A THING
THAT COULD HAPPEN
TO THE BEST OF US.

CORKMEN

AND

NORTHERNERS

ARE THE HARDEST TO HANG

...THEY'VE GOT SUCH

THICK NECKS.

NOSTALGIA FOR
GEORGIAN DUBLIN
IS ALL RIGHT WHEN
YOU DON'T HAPPEN
TO HAVE LIVED IN
ONE OF THOSE RELICS
OF A KING OF ENGLAND.

I LOVE THE SEA—
BUT A DAY IN THE COUNTRY
IS A BLOODY LONG TIME.

●

THE DOCTOR TELLS ME
THAT I HAVE A LIVER
LIKE A HOBNAILED BOOT.

An aunt of mine went to the GPO
on Easter Monday 1916
when the fighting was going on.
She refused to get away and kept
demanding to see her husband.
He finally came to a sandbagged
window and roared
'Go away Maggie',
and she shouted back
'I only wanted to know
if you are going to your
work in the morning.'

SAMUEL BECKETT
IS AN OLD AND GOOD
FRIEND OF MINE,
HE'S ALSO A
MARVELLOUS PLAYWRIGHT.
I DON'T KNOW
WHAT HIS PLAYS ARE ABOUT
BUT I ENJOY THEM.

A CLUB IN CANADA
HAS OFFERED ME
A THOUSAND DOLLARS
TO GO UP THERE AND SING

—FOR DOING THE SAME
IN DUBLIN
I GET THROWN OUT OF PUBS.

I ALWAYS CARRY GELIGNITE;

DYNAMITE ISN'T SAFE.

THE ONLY MAN
I EVER HEARD ADMIT
THAT HE'D BEEN IN THE
BLACK AND TANS
WAS A LIVERPOOL FELLA WHO
EXPLAINED THAT HE JOINED
BECAUSE HE HADN'T
THE FARE FOR THE
FOREIGN LEGION.

THERE WAS A
FELLOW IN PRISON
WHOSE LAWYER WAS
KNOWN TO BOAST
THAT HE GOT HIM
A SUSPENDED SENTENCE.

THEY HANGED HIM.

NOWADAYS
YOU'D ALMOST
BE NEEDING TO
GO TO JAIL
BEFORE YOU'D BE
ACCEPTED AS A
BLOODY WRITER.

CATHOLICS
KEEP A
BETTER TYPE
OF GHOST.

I REGARD
IRELAND
IN THE SAME WAY AS
SEAN O'CASEY.

IT'S A GREAT COUNTRY
TO GET A LETTER FROM.

THE GREAT THING I HAVE DISCOVERED ABOUT ORANGEMEN IS THAT THEY HAVE FEELINGS.

QUEEN VICTORIA
DID ONE GOOD THING
DURING THE IRISH FAMINE
– SHE GAVE FIVE POUNDS TO
THE RELIEF FUND.

BUT SO AS NOT TO
CAUSE JEALOUSY
SHE GAVE FIVE POUNDS
ON THE SAME DAY TO
BATTERSEA DOG'S HOME.

I'M ONLY STAYING ALIVE
TO SAVE FUNERAL EXPENSES.

•

IF I AM ANYTHING AT ALL,
I AM A MAN OF LETTERS.

•

A JOB IS
DEATH WITHOUT DIGNITY.

IN RELIGION
MY FAMILY HAS ALWAYS BEEN
CATHOLIC—AND ANTI-CLERICAL.

•

I HAVE NEVER GIVEN UP THE FAITH
(FOR WHAT WOULD I GIVE IT UP FOR?)

•

WILD HORSES
WOULDN'T DRAG ME BACK TO
THE BOTTLE NOW.

WELL IF I'M A SNOB,
I'M A WORKING-CLASS SNOB,
AND THAT'S THE
BEST KIND OF SNOB.

FOR THE
LOVE AND HONOUR
OF JAYSUS,
LET'S GET OUT OF HERE
AND HAVE A JAR.

THE SIGHT
I'D LIKE TO SEE MOST
IN SPAIN IS
FRANCO'S FUNERAL.

I'M A
COMMUNIST BY DAY,
AND A CATHOLIC
AS SOON AS
IT GETS DARK.

MY GRANDMOTHER
TOOK A BATH
EVERY YEAR,
WHETHER SHE WAS
DIRTY OR NOT.

MESSAGE?
MESSAGE?
WHAT THE HELL
DO YOU THINK I AM,
A BLOODY POSTMAN?

(on being asked 'What was the message of your play?' after a performance of The Hostage*)*

BIBLIOGRAPHY

Behan, Beatrice, *My Life with Brendan* (London: Leslie Frewin, 1965).

Behan, Dominic, *My Brother Brendan* (London: Leslie Frewin, 1961).

Hannigan, Dave, *Behan in the USA* (Bray, Co. Wicklow: Ballpoint Press, 2014).

Jeffs, Rae, *Brendan Behan: Man and Showman* (London: Hutchinson, 1966).

McCann, Sean, (Editor), *The Wit of Brendan Behan* (London: Leslie Frewin, 1969).

Mikhail, E. H., *Brendan Behan: Interviews and Recollections* (2 Vols.) (London: Macmillan, 1982).

O'Connor, Ulick, *Brendan Behan* (London: Hamish Hamilton, 1970)